11/08
25.95

EXPLORING OUR SOLAR SYSTEM

ICE DWARFS

PLUTO AND BEYOND

DAVID JEFFERIS

Crabtree Publishing Company

www.crabtreebooks.com

■THE ICE DWARFS

Ice dwarfs are space objects that **orbit** in the outer **solar system**, beyond the planet Neptune. The best known ice dwarf is Pluto, which used to be regarded as the furthest planet. But in 2005, the slightly bigger world of Eris was discovered, and now Pluto and Eris are called ice dwarfs, or plutoids.

In fact, ice dwarfs are just one of many kinds of chilly object in these distant regions. Together, they are called Trans-Neptunian Objects, or **TNOs**. You will also read about **comets**, icy "snowballs" drifting through space.

Crabtree Publishing Company

PMB 16A,
350 Fifth Avenue, Suite 3308
New York, NY 10118

616 Welland Avenue,
St. Catharines, Ontario
L2M 5V6

Published by Crabtree
Publishing Company
© 2009

Written and produced by:
    David Jefferis/Buzz Books
Educational advisor:
    Julie Stapleton
Science advisor:
    Mat Irvine FBIS
Editor: Molly Aloian
Copy editor: Adrianna Morganelli
Proofreaders: Crystal Sikkens
    Margaret Amy Salter
Project coordinator: Robert Walker
Production coordinator:
    Katherine Kantor
Prepress technicians:
    Margaret Amy Salter
    Katherine Kantor

Note: We have been as accurate as possible with measurements in this book. But TNOs are far away, so many figures are subject to change, usually because of new observations made with improved equipment.

Library and Archives Canada Cataloguing in Publication

Jefferis, David
        Ice dwarfs : Pluto and beyond / David Jefferis.

(Exploring our solar system)
Includes index.
ISBN 978-0-7787-3736-0 (bound).--ISBN 978-0-7787-3752-0 (pbk.)

        1. Pluto (Dwarf planet)--Juvenile literature.   2. Dwarf planets--Juvenile literature.   I. Title.   II. Series: Exploring our solar system (St. Catharines, Ont.)

QB698.J43 2008   j523.4   C2008-904467-3

■ **ACKNOWLEDGEMENTS**
We wish to thank all those people who have helped to create this publication. Information and images were supplied by:

Agencies and organizations:
    ANU Australian National University
    Caltech California Institute of Technology
    ESA European Space Agency
    ESO European Southern Observatory
    HST Hubble Space Telescope
    JPL Jet Propulsion Laboratory
    John Hopkins University Applied Physics Lab
    NASA National Aeronautics and Space Administration
    NASA/Donald E. Davis, Adolph Schaller
    NSSDC National Space Science Data Center

Collections and individuals:
    Alpha Archive
    Comet orbit diagram based on work by
        Larry Koehn, Sky & Telescope magazine
    Comet West picture by Peter Stättmayer
    iStockPhoto/Antonis Papantoniou
    Pluto and Charon picture by:
        M.W. Buie (Lowell Observatory),
        D.J. Tholen (University of Hawaii),
        K. Horne (St. Andrews)

Library of Congress Cataloging-in-Publication Data

Jefferis, David.
    Ice dwarfs : Pluto and beyond / David Jefferis.
        p. cm. -- (Exploring our solar system)
    Includes index.
    ISBN-13: 978-0-7787-3752-0 (pbk. : alk. paper)
    ISBN-10: 0-7787-3752-7 (pbk. : alk. paper)
    ISBN-13: 978-0-7787-3736-0 (reinforced lib. bdg. : alk. paper)
    ISBN-10: 0-7787-3736-5 (reinforced lib. bdg. : alk. paper)
    1. Trans-Neptunian objects--Juvenile literature. 2. Dwarf planets--Juvenile literature. 3. Comets--Juvenile literature. I. Title. II. Series.

    QB694.J44 2009
    523.49--dc22

                                                2008030908

CONTENTS

■ WHAT LIES BEYOND THE PLANETS?

The furthest parts of the solar system are home to countless billions of space objects called TNOs.

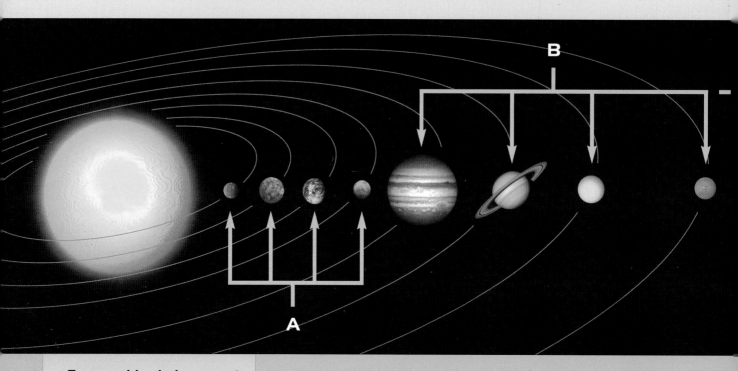

■ **Four worlds circle nearest the Sun. From left to right, they are the small, rocky planets (A) Mercury, Venus, Earth, Mars. Beyond them are four much bigger** gas giants **(B) Jupiter, Saturn, Uranus, Neptune. Beyond these are TNOs (C).**

■ WHAT EXACTLY ARE TNOs?

Basically, anything that orbits the Sun beyond the planet Neptune is called a Trans-Neptunian Object, or TNO. However, there are many different kinds of TNOs. For example, Eris and Pluto are also known as ice dwarfs, or plutoids. Other strange names include **Kuiper Belt** Objects (KBOs), Scattered Disk Objects (SDOs), and **Oort Cloud** Objects (OCOs)!

■ AND WHERE ARE THESE OBJECTS LOCATED?

The various space objects are grouped according to their distance from the Sun. The Kuiper Belt lies beyond Neptune. Beyond this is the Scattered Disk, while furthest away is the Oort Cloud. This is thought to be a vast sphere around the Sun and planets, containing billions of drifting comets—frozen mixtures of rock, gravel, ice, and dust.

C

1 2 3 4

5 6 7 8

ARE TNOs VERY BIG?

Eris, the biggest known TNO, is about half the size of Mercury, the planet nearest the Sun. However, only a few TNOs are anywhere near as large as Eris or Pluto—but there could be many more awaiting discovery.

WOW!
The planets and TNOs move around the Sun in curving paths called orbits. **Moons** also move in orbits, but these circle around their parent planet or TNO.

WHAT ARE THEY MADE OF?

TNOs are much too far away to study closely, so we don't know many details. But it's likely that smaller TNOs are loose mixtures of ice and rock. Bigger TNOs probably have more rock in their makeup.

Here are the biggest known TNOs compared with the much larger Earth, shown to scale below them.

1 Eris (1 moon)
2 Pluto (3 moons)
3 2005 FY9
4 2003 EL61 (2 moons)
5 Sedna
6 Orcus
7 Quaoar
8 Varuna

■WHAT DOES THE TNO SPACE ZONE LOOK LIKE?

TNOs orbit beyond Neptune, in the vast gulf between the Sun and the nearest stars. Here, it is very dark, and very, very cold.

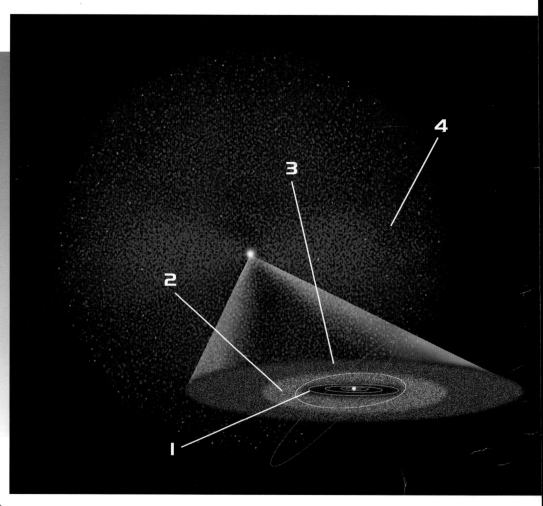

■ This is what we think lies past Neptune's orbit (1).

The Kuiper Belt (2) may contain more than 70,000 objects bigger than 62 miles (100 km) across.

The Scattered Disk (3) has fewer space objects.

The Oort Cloud (4) contains billions of comets. But space is big—you could probably cross the Oort Cloud without seeing a single one!

WOW!
The Scattered Disk gets its name because Neptune's **gravity** scatters some objects away from the nearer Kuiper Belt. Some scientists think the Disk is just an extended Kuiper Belt.

■ HOW FAR DOES TNO SPACE EXTEND?

A long way! In fact, distances are so vast that astronomers use Astronomical Units (**AU**), instead of miles. An AU is the average distance between Earth and the Sun, some 93 million miles (150 million km). Using this scale, the planet Neptune is about 30 AU from the Sun, the Kuiper Belt extends 55 AU, the Scattered Disk about 100 AU and, the Oort Cloud perhaps as far as 50,000 AU.

■ WHERE DID THE TNOs COME FROM?

We think the solar system formed from a vast cloud of gas, dust, and rocks drifting in space. Over billions of years some parts of the cloud coalesced, or joined together, to form a group of young stars—and our Sun was one of these.

Around the Sun was a vast disk of material, which eventually formed into the major planets. Beyond these was the leftover material—today's Trans-Neptunian Objects.

■ The solar system probably looked much like this about 4.6 billion years ago.

Planets that formed near the Sun were small and rocky. Planets that formed further away became the four gas giants.

Beyond the planets lies a vast shell of material that drifts through space today.

■ HOW OLD ARE THEY?

Like the Sun and the planets, TNOs are thought to have formed some 4.6 billion years ago. TNOs are really cosmic rubble that never formed into a major planet.

■ COULD THERE BE AN EARTH-SIZED "PLANET X"?

Well, there might be—but no one has found it yet! Eris is the biggest known TNO, but some astronomers are hunting for a larger, Earth-sized planet.

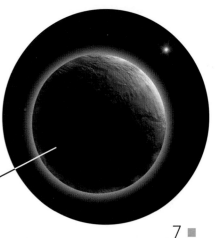

A mystery planet could look like this

■HOW FAR AWAY IS PLUTO?

It's a long way from the Sun, with an oval orbit that varies
from a distant 30 AU, to an even further 49 AU.

■ Charon hangs low in the sky in this view of what Pluto's surface might look like. The snowdrifts are frozen layers of nitrogen, methane, and carbon monoxide.

■ HOW BRIGHT IS THE SUN FROM PLUTO?

The Sun is so far away that it looks about the size of a distant street light. Even so, it's about 300 times brighter than a full moon on Earth, so there's enough light to see with.

■ HOW COLD IS THE SURFACE OF PLUTO?

Since Pluto orbits most of the time far beyond the planet Neptune, it's not surprising that it's a deep-freeze world. Surface temperatures are about -382° F (-230° C).

WOW!
The planets have near-circular orbits. But Pluto's 248 Earth-year orbit is more of an oval shape—from 1979 to 1999, it took Pluto nearer the Sun than Neptune.

◼ IS THERE AN ATMOSPHERE?

Yes, but its **atmosphere** is very thin and only exists when Pluto is nearer the Sun. Then the slight extra heat is enough to turn some of the surface ices to gas. When Pluto moves away from the Sun, these gases freeze again, to fall as snow.

◼ Pluto's surface (1) is covered with ice. Under this are probably layers of water-ice (2). The core (3) may still be hot, a leftover from the fierce heat of the solar system's birth. If so, some of the water-ice may have formed an underground liquid-water ocean.

◼ HOW MANY MOONS ARE IN ORBIT AROUND PLUTO?

There are three known moons: Charon, Nix, and Hydra. At some 750 miles (1,205 km) across, Charon is by far the biggest, as both Nix and Hydra are only about 60 miles (100 km) across. Billions of years ago, Charon and Pluto could have been separate worlds that collided in space. The impact was massive, but not quite enough to shatter either of them. Instead, Pluto and Charon went into orbit around each other, much like Earth and its single, massive Moon.

◼ A cosmic collision between Charon and Pluto could have looked like this. For a short while, temperatures at the impact point would have been hotter than the surface of the distant Sun.

■ WHEN WILL WE SEE PLUTO IN CLOSE-UP?

The New Horizons space probe will fly past Pluto in the year 2015. Then it should give us the first close-up views of this distant place.

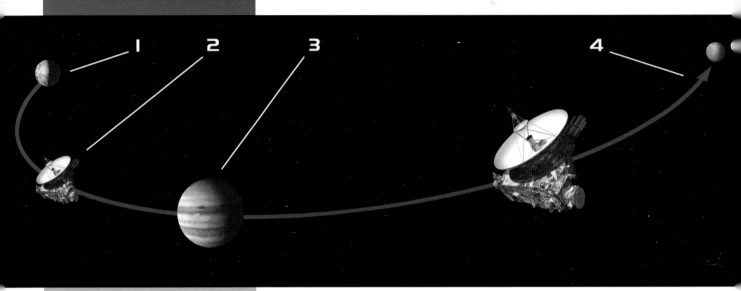

■ The New Horizons space probe was launched from Earth (1) in January 2006. The probe (2) flew past Jupiter (3) 13 months later. The trip to Pluto (4), will have been a flight lasting more than nine years.

■ HOW CLOSE TO PLUTO WILL THE PROBE GO?

The swoop past Pluto will take the probe within 6,000 miles (9,656 km) of Pluto's ultra-cold surface. But the New Horizons photoshoot begins in 2014, a year before fly-by, when its cameras start snapping pictures of Pluto and Charon. The busiest part of the mission will be the final 24 hours as New Horizons hurtles toward Pluto.

WOW!
Compared with the Earth, Pluto is a very small world, with a low gravity pull. A 100 pound (45.5 kg) weight on Earth would weigh just 6.7 pounds (3.03 kg) on Pluto.

■ WHAT WILL THE PROBE SEE?

The cameras can show objects as small as 300 feet (92 m) across, so much of Pluto and its moons should be mapped during the fly-by.

Pluto compared in size to Earth

■ WILL NEW HORIZONS GO ANYWHERE ELSE?

The New Horizons mission will not end with Pluto. The craft will fly on, deep into the Kuiper Belt. It may be able to fly near other TNOs, but at present scientists are still looking for any that are near enough to the probe's flight path.

A good target would be the plutoid Eris, but it will not be near enough for the probe to make a close approach.

■ The half-ton (465 kg) New Horizons probe will speed past Pluto at nearly eight miles per second (13 km/sec).

The onboard instruments will have less than a day to make close-up studies of Pluto and Charon. After that, New Horizons will speed on through the Kuiper Belt.

■ HOW BIG IS ERIS?

The distant ice dwarf Eris is about 1554 miles (2500 km) across. This is about half the size of the smallest planet, Mercury.

■ Eris seems to be mostly a grayish color. This is because methane on the surface stays completely frozen, covering up the differently colored materials lying underneath.

■ HOW FAR FROM THE SUN IS ERIS?

Eris is the most distant solar system object astronomers have measured. At present, Eris is nearly at its furthest distance from the Sun, some 97.5 AU. Astronomers calculate that its oval orbit will one day take it much nearer, to within 38 AU—but that won't be for more than two centuries from now. Being so far from the Sun, Eris takes a long time to complete its long orbit—its "year" actually lasts some 557 Earth-years!

WOW!
Eris is named after a Greek goddess of conflict. But its first name was more fun. The team nicknamed it Xena, after the warrior goddess of a TV series.

■ WHEN WAS ERIS DISCOVERED?

Eris was first spotted by a U.S. team in 2003, although no one realized what it was until 2005. It was found by checking sky pictures for tiny points of light that moved—and Eris was one of these.

Dysnomia

Eris

■ HOW MANY MOONS ORBIT AROUND ERIS?

Eris seems to have just one moon, called Dysnomia. It is thought to be about 93 miles (150 km) across, and orbits Eris at a distance of some 23,240 miles (37,400 km).

Eris and Dysnomia are both incredibly cold—right now, they are so far from the Sun that their temperatures have fallen to about -405° F (-243° C). On this world, you would freeze hard as a block of stone in only a few seconds.

■ Even through a powerful telescope, Eris and its moon Dysnomia (top left) show up only as tiny points of light.

Eris (1 above) moves around the Sun in a highly tilted orbit that takes it far above and below the much flatter orbits of the eight major planets (2) and Pluto (3).

■ If you looked back at the Sun from the Kuiper Belt, the view might look like this. This part of the Belt has a lot of rocks, but most of it probably has far fewer objects.

■WHAT IS SEDNA?

Sedna is another Trans-Neptunian Object. It's presently a little nearer than Eris, but will eventually move much further away into deep space.

■ HOW BIG IS SEDNA COMPARED TO ERIS AND PLUTO?

We don't know its exact size, though it's thought to be a little smaller, perhaps 1,120 miles (1,800 km) across. Sedna is presently approaching its nearest point to the Sun, and is less than 90 AU away. But after the year 2075, it will move outward into space again—to a far-distant 975 AU or more.

■ Sedna's surface could look like this. Much of the ground is colored reddish-brown. This is caused by sunlight, which changes ice, such as methane, into a muddy substance called a tholin.

■ SO DOES SEDNA REALLY BELONG TO THE OORT CLOUD?

Some astronomers think so. It will be far beyond the Kuiper Belt when it reaches its furthest distance furthest from the Sun—but that will not be for another 5,000 years or so. Sedna has the longest solar system orbit found so far, with a "year" that lasts more than 10,000 Earth-years!

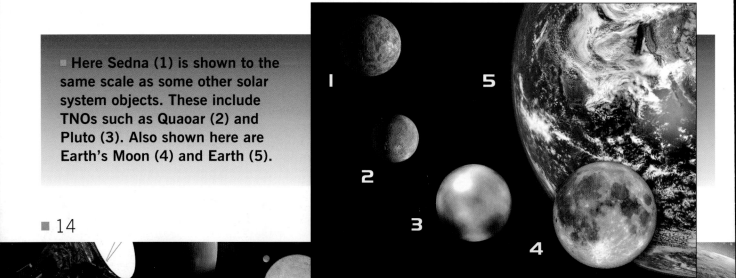

■ Here Sedna (1) is shown to the same scale as some other solar system objects. These include TNOs such as Quaoar (2) and Pluto (3). Also shown here are Earth's Moon (4) and Earth (5).

■ WHY DOES SEDNA HAVE SUCH A DISTANT ORBIT?

The most likely explanation is that Sedna was nudged from a lonely path through the Oort Cloud by a close pass from another star or planet—perhaps even the mysterious "Planet X" that still awaits discovery. We don't know if Sedna has any moons or not, but we do know how long it takes to rotate. A day on Sedna lasts for about 10 hours.

■ This view of Sedna shows a surface with few craters like the huge ones that scar Earth's Moon. Tholins tint much of the landscape red.

From Sedna, the Sun casts hardly more heat than a bright star. And the Sun is so tiny that you could cover it with the head of a pin held at arm's length!

■WHAT IS A COMET?

A comet is a frozen mixture of ice, dust, and rock. Most comets drift through space in the outer solar system, beyond the planets.

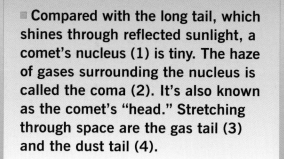

4

3

1

2

■ Compared with the long tail, which shines through reflected sunlight, a comet's nucleus (1) is tiny. The haze of gases surrounding the nucleus is called the coma (2). It's also known as the comet's "head." Stretching through space are the gas tail (3) and the dust tail (4).

■ HOW BIG IS A COMET?

The main part of a comet is the icy nucleus. It is usually less than 30 miles (48 km) across. Most of the time—often for thousands of years—the nucleus is dark and cold. It is invisible to even powerful telescopes.

WOW!
The word comet comes from an ancient Greek word, meaning "hairy one." Comets were thought to bring bad luck, perhaps because of their mysterious arrival.

■ SO HOW CAN WE EVER SEE A COMET?

Comets become visible if they pass near the Sun. Then the Sun's rays start to melt the icy mass of the nucleus. Soon the nucleus may be surrounded by a thin cloud of gas and dust, called the coma, which stretches out to form a long tail.

HOW LONG IS A COMET TAIL?

The size and length varies from comet to comet, but tails are often million of miles long. In fact, there are usually two comet tails, one made of gas, and one of dust. However, even a very bright tail does not contain much matter. You could pack the contents of a million-mile tail into a large suitcase!

These pictures show how a comet's tail grows as it nears the Sun, then shrinks as the comet goes back into deep space again. These pictures are of Halley's comet, a regular visitor that returns every 76 years.

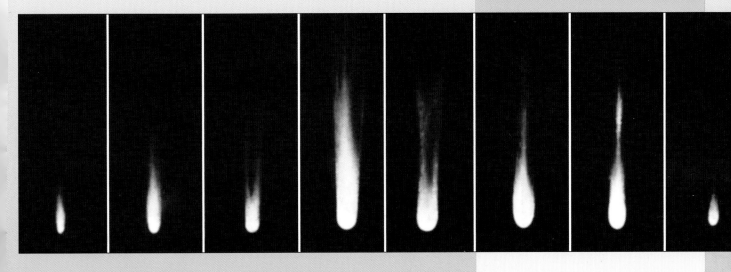

HOW MANY COMETS ARE THERE?

There's no exact answer to this question, but it's likely that there are billions of them. We see very few comets because the only visible ones are those that approach the Sun near enough to develop a glowing tail.

IN WHAT DIRECTION DOES A COMET'S TAIL GO?

Solar particles—called the "solar wind"—blow the tail away from the Sun. So an approaching comet's tail streams behind it. But when the comet is heading out into deep space again, its tail streams ahead.

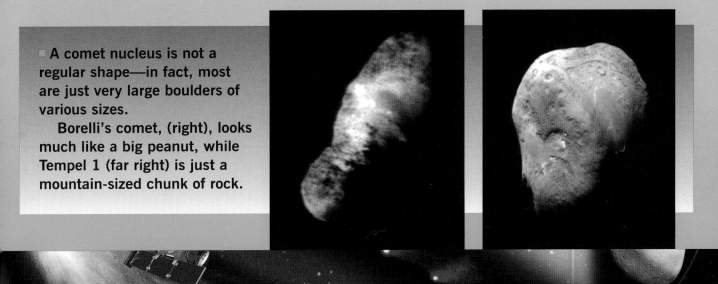

A comet nucleus is not a regular shape—in fact, most are just very large boulders of various sizes.

Borelli's comet, (right), looks much like a big peanut, while Tempel 1 (far right) is just a mountain-sized chunk of rock.

■ WHERE DO COMETS COME FROM?

Some comets have orbits that are fairly near the Sun, but many more come from far beyond the planets, deep in the Oort Cloud.

■ This diagram shows how a comet's tail is blown by the solar wind. As it nears the Sun, the tail streams behind. Once past the Sun, the tail streams out in front.

■ ARE THERE DIFFERENT KINDS OF COMETS?

Comets are divided into two main groups, short-**period** and long-period. A period is the length of time it takes to complete one long, looping orbit of the Sun—it's another name for a comet's "year." Short-period comets rarely go beyond the planet Jupiter, and have periods that range from 3.3 to 60 years. Long-period comets may go out as far as 50,000 AU.

WOW!
All comets are named after the first person to spot them. In fact, if you were the first to see a new comet one dark night, it could be named after you!

■ HOW OFTEN DO LONG-PERIOD COMETS APPEAR?

A few new ones appear most years, but with periods that may be thousands of Earth-years long, they are usually first-time sightings. Kohoutek's comet of 1973 will not return for 75,000 years!

The Solar Heliospheric Observatory (SOHO) probe was launched in 1995

■ This picture of a sun-grazer comet (arrowed) was taken by the SOHO space probe. The white area above the Sun is a flare, a huge explosion big enough to swallow up Earth thousands of times over.

■ WHAT ARE SUN-GRAZER COMETS?

Sun-grazers are comets that pass very close to the Sun, sometimes as near as 31,000 miles (50,000 km). At this distance, the Sun's heat is so intense that such a comet may not survive. Smaller comets can break up and come apart, others fall into the Sun. However, comets move fast, and bigger ones may survive several passes. After several such trips, such a comet may look like a piece of burnt charcoal, all its ices boiled away into space.

■WHAT DOES A COMET'S SURFACE LOOK LIKE?

Space probes have shown them to look much like cratered boulders, made of a mixture of rocks, ice, and dust.

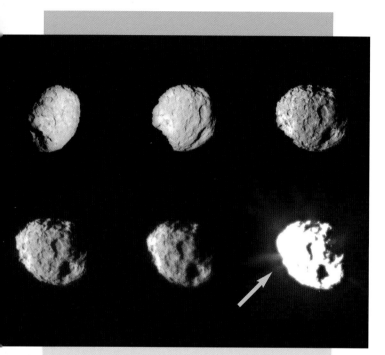

■ **These pictures of comet Wild 2 (pronounced "vilt") were taken by the Stardust probe in 2004.**
   Wild 2's surface was peppered with many cracks and vents that spewed out jets of gas (arrowed) into space, to form the comet's coma.

■ HAVE SPACE PROBES BEEN TO VISIT A COMET?

Comets have been targets for space probes since 1986, when Halley's comet became visible again after 76 years in the outer solar system. Since then, several probes have flown close to comets on fly-by missions. The U.S. Stardust space probe even managed to return samples from the tail of comet Wild 2.

■ HOW CLOSE HAS A PROBE ACTUALLY BEEN TO A COMET?

None have landed on one, but the U.S. Deep Impact space probe went very close to comet Tempel 1 in 2005. It then launched a "penetrator probe" at the comet, to kick up a lot of material from Tempel 1's lumpy surface.

WOW!
Stardust flew through Wild 2's tail at some 13,670 mph (22,000 km/h). The probe captured millions of comet particles that were smaller than grains of sand.

■ WAS DEEP IMPACT A SUCCESS ?

The penetrator probe's impact blew out a crater more than 300 feet (91 m) across. Gas and dust spewed out from the crater for 13 days afterward. Much of the comet's makeup was very fine, like talcum powder, plus water-ice and various kinds of clay. Tempel 1 wasn't a solid body though—much of it was empty space, similar to the texture of snow.

■ The Stardust space probe flew through the tail of comet Wild 2. It took photos and returned samples of the dust tail back to Earth.

■ The samples returned to Earth in a special return capsule. This was sealed to stop the dust from being polluted by contact with Earth's air.

■ From close up, the surface of a comet probably looks like this. All around, jets of gas and dust are pouring from cracks and holes in the surface. Yet once the comet has passed the Sun, the surface will become frozen and motionless again.

■ARE COMETS DANGEROUS?

Normally, the answer is no. But if a comet crashes into a planet, it can cause immense destruction.

Earth to scale

Comet impact zone

■ HAVE WE SEEN A COMET CRASH?

Yes—in 1994, astronomers watched the comet Shoemaker-Levy 9 (SL9) hurtle into the atmosphere of the solar system's biggest planet, the gas giant Jupiter.

Comet SL9 had broken into pieces two years before, so there was not one collision, but 21 of them. The pieces punched huge dark spots in Jupiter's clouds—the biggest one was an immense 7,450 miles (12,000 km) across!

□ SL9's impacts left huge "bruises" in Jupiter's clouds. The scars lasted for months after the collision.

□ A comet strike on Earth may have ended the age of dinosaurs, 65 million years ago. The impact could have changed the climate by filling the sky with dust.

WOW!
Will another huge comet hit our planet? The U.S. Near Earth Object (NEO) Program aims to track the movements of any space objects that might become a danger.

■ HOW OFTEN DO COLLISIONS HAPPEN?

Today, not very often—SL9 was the first time we had seen such an event. However, billions of years ago things were different. There were vast amounts of debris in space, material left over from the solar system's formation. If you look at the Moon on a clear night, you can see many huge craters punched into its surface by these ancient events.

▪ WHAT WAS THE TUNGUSKA EVENT?

In 1908, a massive explosion blasted the air over Siberia in Russia, with the force of at least 1,000 atomic bombs. It could have been caused by a comet colliding with Earth.

▪ DID THE EVENT CAUSE DAMAGE?

At that time, the area had few towns or people in it, so the damage was mostly to Siberia's immense forests. Some 80 million trees were flattened, over an area of more than 800 square miles (2,071 sq km).

▪ The space view (above) shows pieces of a broken-up comet heading for our planet. The chunks glow red with the heat caused by slamming into the atmosphere at up to 37 miles per second (60 km/sec).

The Tunguska event (below) was the biggest of its kind in recent history.

■WHAT ARE ASTEROIDS AND METEOROIDS?

Asteroids **are rocky space objects, most of which orbit the Sun in a big group called the Asteroid Belt.** Meteoroids **are drifting chunks of rock or metal.**

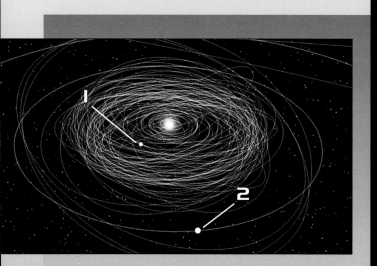

■ Most of the asteroids (marked above in yellow) circle the Sun in a belt between Mars (1) and Jupiter (2).
   Most asteroids are odd-shaped chunks of rock, like 8 mile-long (13 km) Eros (right).

■ HOW ARE ASTEROIDS AND METEOROIDS DIFFERENT?

There's no single definition, but an asteroid is usually reckoned to be any Sun-orbiting chunk of rock that's "bigger than a boulder," about 150 feet (46 m) across. Anything below this size is called a meteoroid.

■ WHAT IS THE BIGGEST ASTEROID?

Its name is Ceres, and it's big enough to be deemed officially as a dwarf planet. At some 590 miles (950 km) across, Ceres is by far the biggest object in the main Asteroid Belt – it contains about one-third of all the matter orbiting between Mars and Jupiter.

WOW!
The Dawn space probe was launched in 2007 to explore the Asteroid Belt. Its first target will be Ceres. After that, Dawn will fly on to explore Vesta.

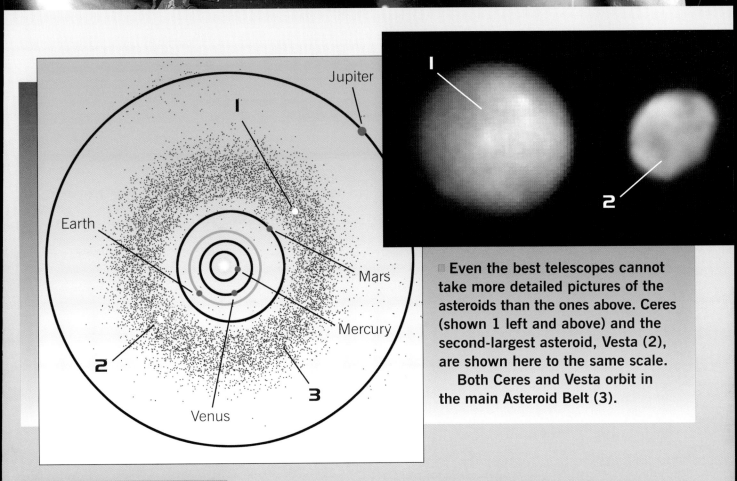

Jupiter

I

Earth

2

Venus

Mars

Mercury

3

Even the best telescopes cannot take more detailed pictures of the asteroids than the ones above. Ceres (shown 1 left and above) and the second-largest asteroid, Vesta (2), are shown here to the same scale.

Both Ceres and Vesta orbit in the main Asteroid Belt (3).

A rain of meteoroids crosses the Earth's orbit, and some of these fall through the atmosphere as brightly glowing meteors, but only a few ever hit the ground.

Meteor Crater in the U.S. (below) was punched out 50,000 years ago by a 150-foot (46-m) meteor.

IS CERES REALLY LIKE A SMALL PLANET?

Ceres is called a dwarf planet because of its size, and the fact that it is sphere-shaped, like a planet such as Earth. The surface is probably made of water-ice, minerals, and clays. Below this could be a hidden ocean of liquid water.

Ceres may even have a very thin atmosphere, perhaps with water vapor, making it a possible—though unlikely—home for **alien** life. The Dawn space probe should find out more.

■ WHAT CAN I SEE FROM EARTH?

Only super powerful telescopes can hunt for TNOs. Even then, they appear only as tiny points of light. But you can spot meteors and comets easily.

■ WHAT EQUIPMENT DO I NEED FOR METEOR SPOTTING?

If you plan to look for one of the meteor showers listed opposite, then allow for at least an hour or two of sky-watching. Binoculars are handy for looking at the Moon if it's visible, and a lightweight folding chair can be useful. Remember that even in summer, nights can be chilly, so take warm clothes and a pair of gloves.

■ WHERE ARE THE BEST VIEWING POINTS?

Most of us live in towns and cities, which is a pity, because street lighting is the enemy of astronomy—many faint sky objects are drowned out by the glare of the lights. If you can, a good idea is to make a trip to the countryside, where nights are darker. Then you'll have a good chance of seeing the streaks of meteors as they whizz across the sky.

■ Meteor showers appear to be coming from one part of the sky, called the radiant.

Showers are named for their radiant. So the Perseids, for example, seem to come from the constellation (or star group) called Perseus.

■ A really big comet may appear in the sky for weeks or months. Such comets are easy to see without equipment, and are usually such big news events that you cannot miss them.

■ WHAT DO METEORS LOOK LIKE?

Meteors hit the upper atmosphere at up to 45 miles per second (72 km/sec), when the intense heat of air friction at that speed burns them to dust. We see the glow of their fiery end as a brief streak of light across the sky.

Meteors often come in "showers" over several nights. Many of these are thought to be the remains of dead comets that move in streams across the solar system. When Earth passes through such a stream, we see a shower.

■ AND WHAT ABOUT COMETS?

As for comets, only a few are ever visible without using binoculars or a telescope—and then the view can be tremendous. But big comets are rare, and appear in our skies only every few years.

WOW!
In 1910, Earth went through the tail of Halley's comet. Reports of poison gases in the tail worried many people—but any gases were so thin that there was no danger.

■ Here are some meteor showers linked to comets. They mostly appear on or around these dates every year. The comets' names are shown in brackets.

Lyrids (186 II)
April 22
Eta Aquarids (Halley)
May 6
Perseids (186 III)
August 12
Draconids (Giacobini-Zinner)
October 9
Orionids (Halley)
October 21
Taurids (Encke)
November 5
Leonids (Tempel)
November 17
Ursids (Tuttle)
December 22

■ FACTS AND FIGURES

■ ERIS STATISTICS

Diameter

About 1,550 miles (2,500 km), making Eris the ninth biggest object in the solar system, after Mercury, the smallest planet.

Time to rotate ("day")

Eris is thought to turn once every eight hours.

Time to orbit once around the Sun ("year")

Eris completes one orbit of the Sun every 557 Earth-years.

Distance to the Sun

The orbit of Eris ranges from 37.8 AU (nearest the Sun) to 97.6 (furthest).

Composition

Frozen surface, interior likely to be made up of a rock-and-ice mixture.

Temperature

The average surface temperature is about -384° F (-231° C).

Surface gravity

Here on Earth we live under a force of one gravity, or 1G. Eris is less massive than our planet, and has a gravity pull about 12 times less.

Atmosphere

There may be traces of methane gas when Eris is nearest the Sun. At other times, the gas remains frozen on the surface.

Moons

Eris has a single moon, Dysnomia. It has a diameter of about 219 miles (352 km).

■ One of the strangest TNOs is an egg-shaped world, called 2003 EL61, but nicknamed "Santa."

It rotates in less than four hours, which is fast enough to stretch it into the strange oval shape.

Santa has a pair of small moons, which have also got nicknames. They are called "Rudolf" and "Blitzen!"

PLUTO STATISTICS

Diameter

Pluto is just 1,485 miles (2,390 km) across.

Time to rotate ("day")

Pluto turns slowly, just once every six days, nine hours, 17 minutes.

Time to orbit once around the Sun ("year")

Pluto's orbit is 248 Earth-years long.

Distance to the Sun

Pluto's orbit ranges from 29.7 AU to 49.3 AU.

Composition

A frozen surface with an interior likely to be a rock-and-ice mixture.

Temperature

Pluto's average surface temperature is about -382° F (-230° C).

Surface gravity

About 16 times less than Earth's gravity.

Atmosphere

Pluto's atmosphere is a thin covering of nitrogen, methane, and carbon monoxide. As Pluto moves away from the Sun, these gases slowly freeze again and fall to the ground as snow.

Moons

Pluto has three moons. The biggest is Charon, at 749 miles (1,205 km) across. The two smaller moons are called Nix and Hydra.

■ The TNO Quaoar (right) was discovered in 2002. Like other TNOs it was named after a god from an early myth, in this case one of a Native American tribe. Other TNO names include Eris, which comes from ancient Greece. Pluto was the Roman god of the underworld. Sedna is an Inuit goddess of the sea.

■GLOSSARY

Here are explanations for many of the terms used in this book.

■ Comet Hale-Bopp shows its gas and dust tails during the passage of 1997.

Alien The name for life that might exist other than on Earth. So far, none has been found.

Asteroid One of many space rocks, mostly orbiting in a large belt between the planets Mars and Jupiter.

Atmosphere The layers of gases surrounding a planet or big TNO.

AU Astronomical Unit, the average distance from Earth to the Sun, 93 million miles (150 million km).

Carbon monoxide A colourless gas, formed in many ways, from volcanic eruptions to vehicle exhausts.

Comet A space "snowball," made of a mixture of dust, gas, and rock. When near the Sun, the heat produces a long, shining tail.

Constellation One of 88 star-patterns in the sky, named by the ancient Greeks and Romans.

Core The center of a planet or a big TNO such as Eris or Pluto.

Gas giant A large planet made mostly of gases with no solid surface, such as Jupiter. Rocky worlds or moons have a hard crust you could walk on.

Gravity The universal force of attraction between all objects.

Ice dwarf An icy space object that orbits the Sun past Neptune. Pluto and Eris are ice dwarfs, but are also known by the official name, plutoid.

Kuiper Belt (pronounced Ky-per Belt). The vast halo of space objects that circles the Sun past the planets. Beyond this is the Scattered Disk, made of objects flung from the Kuiper Belt by the effects of Neptune's gravity.

Meteor, meteoroid A chunk of space rock, which can be stony, rocky or metal. If a meteoroid hits Earth's atmosphere it usually burns up in a few seconds, then it is called a meteor. If a piece survives to hit the ground, it is then called a meteorite.

Methane A colorless, flammable gas. On Earth, it is the main part of natural gas used for heating homes.

Moon A space object that orbits around a planet, TNO, or other larger space object.

■ The NEAR Shoemaker space probe landed on the asteroid Eros in 2001. Close-up pictures showed a pitted and rocky surface.

Part of the Sun to the same scale as the planets

1 2 3 4 5 6 7 8

Nitrogen Colorless substance found in living things, and as a gas in Earth's atmosphere. Various TNOs are covered with frozen nitrogen.

Oort Cloud The vast cloud of comets that surrounds the solar system.

Orbit The curving path a space object takes around a more massive one, such as a planet orbiting the Sun, or a moon moving around a planet.

Period Another name for the length of a space object's "year," the length of time it takes to circle the Sun once.

Radiant Part of the sky from which a meteor shower seems to come.

Solar system The name for the Sun and the eight major planets, TNOs, and other space objects that circle it.

Sun-grazer A comet that passes very close to the Sun. The SOHO space observatory has spotted many such comets—by June 2008, it had observed 1500 comets, including many sun-grazers.

Tholin A reddish-brown "mud" that forms when sunlight falls on substances such as nitrogen and methane.

TNO A Trans-Neptunian Object is anything that orbits in space beyond the planet Neptune.

■ Here are the Sun and major planets:
1 Mercury
2 Venus
3 Earth
4 Mars
5 Jupiter
6 Saturn
7 Uranus
8 Neptune

■ GOING FURTHER

Using the Internet is a great way to expand your knowledge of space, ice dwarfs, and comets.

Your first visit should be to the site of the U.S. space agency, NASA. Its site shows almost everything to do with space, from the history of spaceflight to astronomy, and also plans for future missions.

There are also websites that give detailed space information. Try these sites to start with:

http://www.nasa.gov A huge space site.
http://www.space.com Space news site.
http://neo.jpl.nasa.gov/neo Tracking space rocks.
http://www.ifa.hawaii.edu/faculty/jewitt/kb.html
Kuiper Belt information.

■INDEX